In the Year 1954

By

Kerry Butters.

In the Year 1954.

Millennium:	2nd millennium
Centuries:	19th century – **20th century** – 21st century
Decades:	1920s 1930s 1940s – **1950s** – 1960s 1970s 1980s
Years:	1951 1952 1953 – **1954** – 1955 1956 1957

1954 (MCMLIV) was a common year starting on Friday (dominical letter C) of the Gregorian calendar, the 1954th year of the Common Era (CE) and *Anno Domini* (AD) designations, the 954th year of the 2nd millennium, the 54th year of the 20th century, and the 5th year of the 1950s decade.

Contents

- 1 Events
- 2 Births
- 3 Deaths
- 4 Nobel Prizes
- 5 In the News

Events

January

- January 1 – The Soviet Union ceases to demand war reparations from East Germany.
- January 10 – BOAC Flight 781, a de Havilland Comet jet plane, disintegrates in mid-air due to metal fatigue and crashes in the Mediterranean near Elba. All 35 people on board are killed.
- January 12 – Avalanches in Austria kill more than 200.
- January 14 – Marilyn Monroe marries baseball player Joe DiMaggio.
- January 15 – Mau Mau leader Waruhiu Itote is captured in Kenya.
- January 17 – In Yugoslavia, Milovan Đilas, one of the leading members of the League of Communists of Yugoslavia, is relieved of his duties.
- January 20 – The US-based National Negro Network is established with forty-six member radio stations.

- January 21 – The first nuclear-powered submarine, the USS *Nautilus*, is launched in Groton, Connecticut, by First Lady of the United States Mamie Eisenhower.
- January 25 – The foreign ministers of the United States, Britain, France and the Soviet Union meet at the Berlin Conference.

January 14: Marilyn weds DiMaggio.

February

- February 3 – Elizabeth II becomes the first reigning monarch to visit Australia.
- February 10 – After authorizing $385 million over the $400 million already budgeted for military aid to Vietnam, President of the United States Dwight D. Eisenhower warns against his country's intervention in Vietnam.
- February 19 – 1954 transfer of Crimea: The Soviet Politburo of the Soviet Union orders the transfer the Crimean Oblast from the Russian SFSR to the Ukrainian SSR.
- February 23 – The first mass vaccination of children against polio begins in Pittsburgh, United States.
- February 25 – Lt. Col. Gamal Abdel Nasser becomes premier of Egypt.

March

- March 1
  - U.S. officials announce that a hydrogen bomb test (Castle Bravo) has been conducted on Bikini Atoll in the Pacific Ocean.
  - U.S. Capitol shooting incident: Four Puerto Rican nationalists open fire in the United States House of Representatives chamber and wound five; they are apprehended by security guards.
- March 9 – American journalists Edward R. Murrow and Fred W. Friendly produce a 30-minute *See It Now* documentary, entitled *A Report on Senator Joseph McCarthy*.
- March 12 – Finland and Germany officially end their state of war.
- March 13 – French troops begin the battle against the Viet Minh in Dien Bien Phu.
- March 19 – Joey Giardello knocks out Willie Tory at Madison Square Garden, in the first televised boxing prize fight to be shown in colour.
- March 23 – In Vietnam, the Viet Minh capture the main airstrip of Dien Bien Phu. The remaining French Army units there are partially isolated.
- March 25
  - The 26th Academy Awards ceremony is held.
  - RCA manufactures the first color television set (12-inch screen; price: $1,000)
  - The Soviet Union recognises the sovereignty of East Germany. Soviet troops remain in the country.

- March 27 – The Castle Romeo nuclear test explosion is executed.
- March 28
    - Puerto Rico's first television station, *WKAQ-TV*, commences broadcasting.
    - Trial of A. L. Zissu and 12 other Zionist leaders ends with harsh sentences in Communist Romania.
- March 29 – A C-47 transport with French nurse Geneviève de Galard on board is wrecked on the runway at Dien Bien Phu.
- March 30 – The first operational subway line in Canada opens in Toronto.

April

- April – Bill Haley & His Comets record "Rock Around the Clock", thus starting the rock and roll craze.
- April 1
    - The U.S. Congress and President Dwight D. Eisenhower authorize the founding of the United States Air Force Academy in Colorado.
    - South Point School (India) is founded and becomes the largest school in the world by 1992.
- April 3 – Vladimir Petrov defects from the Soviet Union and asks for political asylum in Australia.
- April 4 – The legendary symphony conductor Arturo Toscanini experiences a lapse of memory during a concert. At this concert's end, his retirement is announced, and Toscanini never conducts in public again.

- April 7 – Dwight D. Eisenhower gives his "domino theory" speech during a news conference.
- April 8 – A Royal Canadian Air Force Canadair Harvard collides with a Trans-Canada Air Lines Canadair North Star over Moose Jaw, Saskatchewan, killing 37 people.
- April 11 – This day is denoted as the most boring day in the 20th century by True Knowledge, an answer engine developed by William Tunstall-Pedoe. No significant newsworthy events, births, or deaths are known to have happened on this day.
- April 14
  - Aneurin Bevan resigns from the British Labour Party's "Shadow Cabinet".
  - A Soviet spy ring in Australia is unveiled.
- April 16 – Vice President Richard Nixon announces that the United States may be "putting our own boys in Indochina regardless of Allied support".
- April 22 – Senator Joseph McCarthy begins hearings investigating the United States Army for being "soft" on Communism.
- April 26 –
  - An international conference on Korea and Indo-China opens in Geneva.
  - Akira Kurosawa's *Seven Samurai* is released in Japan.
- April 28 – U.S. Secretary of State John Foster Dulles accuses Communist China of sending combat troops to Indo-China to train the Viet Minh guerrillas.

May

- May 1 – The Unification Church is founded in South Korea.
- May 4 – General Alfredo Stroessner deposes Federico Chávez in a coup d'état in Paraguay; from August 15 he will hold the office of President until 1989.
- May 6 – Roger Bannister runs the first sub-four minute mile, in Oxford, England.
- May 7 – Vietnam War (run-up): The Battle of Dien Bien Phu ends in a French defeat (the battle began on March 13).
- May 8 – The Asian Football Confederation (AFC) is formed in Manila, Philippines.
- May 11 – U.S. Secretary of State John Foster Dulles declares that Indochina is important but not essential to the security of Southeast Asia, thus ending any prospect of American intervention on the side of France.
- May 14
  - The Boeing 707 is released after about two years of development.
  - The Hague Convention for the Protection of Cultural Property in the Event of Armed Conflict was adopted in The Hague, Netherlands.
- May 15 – The Latin Union (*Unión Latina*) is created by the Convention of Madrid. Its member countries use the five Romance languages: Italian, French, Spanish, Portuguese, and Romanian. It will suspend operations in 2012.
- May 17
  - *Brown v. Board of Education* (347 US 483 1954): The U.S. Supreme Court rules unanimously that segregated schools are unconstitutional.

- o The Royal Commission on the Petrov Affair in Australia begins its inquiry.
  - o Adnan Menderes of the Democrat Party forms the new (21st) government of Turkey.
- May 20 – Chiang Kai-shek is reelected as the president of the Republic of China by the National Assembly.
- May 22 – The common Nordic Labour Market act is signed.
- May 26 – A fire on board the U.S. Navy aircraft carrier USS *Bennington* off Narragansett Bay, Massachusetts, kills 103 sailors.
- May 29
  - o Robert Menzies's government is reelected for a fourth term in Australia.
  - o Creation and first meeting of the Bilderberg Group.
  - o Diane Leather becomes the first woman to run a sub-five minute mile, in Birmingham, England.

June

- June 7 – Early computer scientist Alan Turing commits suicide.
- June 9 – McCarthyism: Joseph Welch, special counsel for the United States Army, lashes out at Senator Joseph McCarthy, during hearings on whether Communism has infiltrated the Army, saying, "Have you, at long last, no decency?"
- June 14 – The words "under God" are added to the United States Pledge of Allegiance.
- June 15 – The UEFA (Union of European Football Associations) is formed in Basel, Switzerland.

- June 16 – July 4 – the 1954 FIFA World Cup is held in Switzerland
- June 17 – A CIA-engineered military coup occurs in Guatemala.
- June 18 – Pierre Mendès France becomes prime minister of France.
- June 22
  - Sarah Mae Flemming is expelled from a bus in South Carolina for sitting in a white-only section.
  - Parker–Hulme murder case: 16-year old Pauline Parker and her friend 15-year-old Juliet Hulme bludgeon Parker's mother to death using a brick at Victoria Park in New Zealand.
- June 27
  - Guatemalan President Jacobo Árbenz steps down in a CIA-sponsored military coup, triggering a bloody civil war that continues for more than 35 years.
  - The world's first atomic power station opens at Obninsk, near Moscow.

July

- July 1
  - The Common Nordic Labor Market Act comes into effect.
  - The United States officially begins using the international unit of the nautical mile, equal to 6,076.11549 ft. or 1,852 meters.

- July 4
  - Food rationing in Great Britain ends with the lifting of restrictions on sale and purchase of meat, 14 years after it began early in World War II and nearly a decade after the war's end.
  - "Miracle of Bern": West Germany beats Hungary 3–2 to win the 1954 FIFA World Cup.
- July 10 – Peter Thomson becomes the first Australian to win the British Open Golf Championship.
- July 15
  - The maiden flight of the Boeing 367-80 (or Dash 80), prototype of the Boeing 707 series.
  - Juan Fangio, the Argentine driver for German Grand Prix team Mercedes-Benz, makes a new fastest lap of the Silverstone Circuit with an average speed of 100.35 mph, the previous record being 100.16 mph.
- July 21 – First Indochina War: The Geneva Conference sends French forces to the south, and Vietnamese forces to the north, of a ceasefire line, and calls for elections to decide the government for all of Vietnam by July 1956. Failure to abide by the terms of the agreement leads to the establishment de facto of regimes of North Vietnam and South Vietnam, and the Vietnam War.
- July 31 – Italian mountaineers Lino Lacedelli and Achille Compagnoni become the first successfully to reach the summit of the Himalayan peak K2.

August

- August 1 – The First Indochina War ends with the Vietnam People's Army in North Vietnam, the Vietnamese National Army in South Vietnam, the Kingdom of Cambodia in Cambodia, and the Kingdom of Laos in Laos, emerging victorious against the French Army.
- August 6 – Emilie Dionne, one of the Dionne quintuplets, dies of asphyxiation following an epileptic seizure. She is the first of the five to perish, and three of them live into the 21st century.
- August 16 – The first issue of *Sports Illustrated* magazine is published in the United States.
- August 24 – Brazilian president Getúlio Vargas commits suicide after being accused of involvement in a conspiracy to murder his chief political opponent, Carlos Lacerda.

September

- September 3 – The last 'new' episode of *The Lone Ranger* radio program is broadcast, after 2,956 episodes over a period of 21 years. Reruns of old episodes continue to be transmitted.
- September 6 – The SEATO treaty is signed in Manila, Philippines.
- September 8 – The Southeast Asia Treaty Organization (SEATO) is established in Bangkok, Thailand.
- September 9 – The 6.7 Mw Chlef earthquake shakes northern Algeria with a maximum Mercalli intensity of XI (*Extreme*).

The shock destroyed Orléansville, left 1,243–1,409 dead, and 5,000 injured.
- September 11 – The Miss America Pageant is broadcast on television for the first time.
- September 14
  - The Soviet Union test fires a thermonuclear bomb for the first time.
  - English composer Benjamin Britten's chamber opera version of *The Turn of the Screw* receives its world premiere at the Teatro La Fenice in Venice, Italy.
- September 15 – Black Wednesday in air travel: severe delays to flights due to bad weather along the East Coast of the United States.
- September 17 – William Golding's novel *Lord of the Flies* is published in London.
- September 25 – Footscray Football Club win their first and only Australian Football League Grand Final.
- September 26 – The Japanese ferry *Tōya Maru* sinks during a typhoon in the Tsugaru Strait. More than 1,100 people are killed. Seven other ships are wrecked and at least nine others seriously damaged.
- September 30 – The USS *Nautilus* (SSN-571), the first nuclear-powered submarine in the world, is commissioned into the U.S. Navy.

October

- October 11
  - Pre-Vietnam War: The Viet Minh takes control of North Vietnam.

- Hurricane Hazel crosses over Haiti, killing 1,000.
- October 15 – Hurricane Hazel makes U.S. landfall; it is the only recorded Category 4 hurricane to strike as far north as North Carolina.
- October 18
  - Texas Instruments announces the development of the first commercial transistor radio. The Regency TR-1 goes on sale the following month.
  - The comic strip *Hi and Lois*, by Mort Walker and Dik Browne, is launched.
- October 20 – A dock workers' strike expands in England.
- October 23
  - West Germany joins NATO.
  - Paris Agreement sets up the Western European Union to implement the Treaty of Brussels (1948) providing for mutual self-defence and other collaboration between Belgium, France, West Germany, Italy, Luxembourg, the Netherlands and the United Kingdom.
- October 25 – Landslides caused by heavy rains hit Salerno, Italy, killing about 300.
- October 26 – Muslim Brotherhood member Mahmoud Abdul Latif tries to kill Gamal Abdel Nasser.
- October 31 – Algerian War of Independence: The Algerian National Liberation Front begins a revolt against French rule.

November

- November 1 – The FLN attacks representative and public buildings of the French colonial power.
- November 2
    - The dock workers' strike in the UK comes to an end.
    - The radio program *Hancock's Half Hour*, a pioneer in situation comedy, is first broadcast on BBC Radio. A television version would follow in 1956.
- November 3 – The first *Godzilla* film premieres in Tokyo.
- November 5 – Japan and Burma sign a peace treaty in Rangoon, to end their long-extinct state of war.
- November 10 – U.S. President Dwight D. Eisenhower dedicates the USMC War Memorial (Iwo Jima memorial) at the Arlington National Cemetery.
- November 12 – The main immigration port-of-entry in New York Harbor at Ellis Island closes permanently.
- November 14 – Egyptian president Muhammad Naguib is deposed, and Gamal Abdel Nasser replaces him.
- November 19 – The Korean Cold War between the communist North and the capitalist South begins over a year after the conclusion of the Korean War.
- November 22 – The U.S. Supreme Court decides the landmark case Berman v. Parker (348 U.S. 26), upholding the federal slum clearance and urban renewal programs.
- November 23 – The Dow Jones Industrial Average rises 3.27 points, or 0.86 percent, closing at an all-time high of 382.74. More significantly, this is the first time the Dow has surpassed its peak level reached just before the Wall Street Crash of 1929.

- November 30 – In Sylacauga, Alabama, a four-kilogram piece of the Hodges Meteorite crashes through the roof of a house and badly bruises a napping woman, in the first documented case of an object from outer space hitting a person.

December

- December 1 – The first Hyatt Hotel, The Hyatt House Los Angeles, opens on the grounds of Los Angeles International Airport. It is the first hotel in the world built on an airport property.
- December 2
    - Red Scare: The United States Senate votes 67–22 to condemn Joseph McCarthy for "conduct that tends to bring the Senate into dishonor and disrepute."
    - The Taiwan-United States Mutual Defense Treaty is signed.
- December 4 – The first Burger King opens in Miami, Florida.
- December 15 – The Netherlands Antilles is created out of the Dutch Caribbean nations. It is later dissolved between 1986 and 2010.
- December 23 – J. Hartwell Harrison, and Joseph Murray perform the world's first successful kidney transplant in Boston, Massachusetts.
- December 24 – Laos gains full independence from France.

Date unknown

- New Zealand engineer Sir William Hamilton develops the first pump-jet engine (the "Hamilton Jet") capable of propelling a jetboat.
- The first electric drip brew coffeemaker is patented in Germany and named the Wigomat after its inventor Gottlob Widmann.
- The Boy Scouts of America desegregates on the basis of race.
- Gerbils (*Meriones unguiculatus*) are brought to the United States by Dr. Victor Schwentker.
- The case of Lothar Malskat, who had admitted that he had painted the supposedly antique frescoes in Marienkirche himself, goes to trial.
- The TV dinner is introduced by the American entrepreneur Gerry Thomas.
- New York City Ballet founding balletmaster George Balanchine's production of *The Nutcracker* is staged for the first time in New York City, and it became a tradition there, still being performed annually as of 2010.
- South Korea opens the Gimpo International Airport.
- In South Vietnam the Viet Minh is reorganised into the Viet Cong.
- After the death of Joseph Stalin, the Soviet Union starts releasing political prisoners and deportees from its Gulag prison camps.

Births

January

Howard Stern

Robert F. Kennedy, Jr.

Katey Sagal

Oprah Winfrey

- January 2 – Henry Bonilla, American politician
- January 3 – Ross the Boss, American heavy metal/punk guitarist
- January 4
  - Tina Knowles, Fashion designer; mother of R&B singers Beyoncé and Solange Knowles
  - Dave "The Devilfish" Ulliott, English professional poker player
- January 5 – Alex English, American basketball player
- January 6 – Anthony Minghella, British film and theatre director (d. 2008)
- January 7
  - Jodi Long, American actress
  - José María Vitier, Cuban music composer and pianist
- January 8 – Julieta Castellanos, Honduran sociologist
- January 12 – Howard Stern, American radio host
- January 13 – Trevor Rabin, South African–American musician
- January 14
  - Tom Cheney, American cartoonist
  - Masanobu Fuchi, Japanese professional wrestler
- January 15 – Jose Dalisay, Jr., Filipino writer

- January 17 – Robert F. Kennedy, Jr., American socialite and environmental activist
- January 19
    - Ted DiBiase, American professional wrestler
    - Katey Sagal, American actress and singer
    - Katharina Thalbach, German actress
- January 21 – Thomas de Maizière, German politician
- January 22 – Peter Pilz, Austrian politician
- January 23
    - Franco De Vita, Venezuelan singer and songwriter
    - Edward Ka-Spel, British/Dutch singer-songwriter (The Legendary Pink Dots)
- January 28
    - Bruno Metsu, French football coach (d. 2013)
    - Kaneto Shiozawa, Japanese voice actor (d. 2000)
- January 29
    - Yukinobu Hoshino, Japanese cartoonist
    - Terry Kinney, American actor
    - Oprah Winfrey, American actress, talk show hostess, producer, and publisher

February

John Travolta

Matt Groening

Rene Russo

Recep Tayyip Erdoğan

- February 1 – Bill Mumy, American child actor and musician
- February 2 – Christie Brinkley, American model
- February 7 – Dieter Bohlen, German music producer and singer-songwriter (Modern Talking, Blue System)

- February 9
  - Chris Gardner, American entrepreneur
  - Gina Rinehart, Australian mining tycoon.
  - Kevin Warwick, English cybernetic scientist
- February 11 – Noriyuki Asakura, Japanese composer
- February 12 – Philip Zimmermann, American cryptographer
- February 13 – Donnie Moore, American baseball player (d. 1989)
- February 15 – Matt Groening, American cartoonist
- February 16 – Iain Banks, Scottish author (d. 2013)
- February 17
  - Rene Russo, American actress
  - Yuji Takada, Japanese free-style wrestler
- February 18 – John Travolta, American actor
- February 19 – Messaouda Boubaker, Tunisian writer
  - Sócrates, Brazilian footballer (d. 2011)
- February 20
  - Anthony Head, English actor
  - Patty Hearst, American heiress and kidnapping victim
- February 23 – Viktor Yushchenko, President of Ukraine
- February 25 – Gerardo Pelusso, Uruguayan football manager
- February 26 – Recep Tayyip Erdoğan, 12th President of Turkey

March

Ron Howard

François Fillon

Catherine O'Hara

Robert Carradine

- March 1
  - Catherine Bach, American actress
  - Ron Howard, American actor, director, producer (*The Andy Griffith Show* and *Happy Days*)
- March 2
  - Ed Johnstone, Canadian ice hockey player
  - Gara Takashima, Japanese voice actress
- March 4
  - François Fillon, Prime Minister of France
  - Catherine O'Hara, Canadian actress (*SCTV*)
  - Irina Ratushinskaya, Russian writer
  - Willie Thorne, English snooker player
- March 6 – Harald Schumacher, German football goalkeeper
- March 8
  - Marie-Theres Nadig, Swiss alpine skier
  - David Wilkie, Scottish swimmer
- March 9 – Bobby Sands, Irish republican hunger striker (d. 1981)
- March 13 – The Baroness Amos, British politician
- March 15
  - Massimo Bubola, Italian singer-songwriter
  - Craig Wasson, American actor
- March 16
  - S.A. Griffin, American actor and poet

- o Nancy Wilson, American rock musician
- March 17 – Lesley-Anne Down, British actress
- March 18 – James F. Reilly, American astronaut
- March 19 – Indu Shahani, Indian educator and Sheriff of Mumbai
- March 20 – Louis Sachar, American author
- March 23
  - o Geno Auriemma, American basketball coach
  - o Hideyuki Hori, Japanese voice actor
- March 24
  - o Robert Carradine, American actor
  - o Donna Pescow, American actress and director
- March 26
  - o Kazuhiko Inoue, Japanese voice actor
  - o Clive Palmer, Australian mining tycoon
- March 29 – Karen Ann Quinlan, American right-to-die cause célèbre (d. 1985)

April

Jackie Chan

Dennis Quaid

Jerry Seinfeld

- April 1 – Dieter Müller, German soccer player
- April 2 – Susumu Hirasawa, Japanese musician
- April 5 – Guy Bertrand, Canadian linguist and radio/television personality
- April 6
    - Judi Bowker, English actress
    - Michael Simms (publisher), American poet and publisher; founded Autumn House Press
- April 7
    - Jackie Chan, Hong Kong-born actor
    - Tony Dorsett, American football player
- April 8
    - Gary Carter, American baseball player (d. 2012)
    - John Schneider, American actor (*Dukes of Hazzard*)

- April 9
    - Steve Holt, Canadian musician
    - Dennis Quaid, American actor
- April 10 – Anacani, Mexican-born American singer
- April 14 – Bruce Sterling, American science fiction writer
- April 16 – Ellen Barkin, American actress
- April 17
    - Norio Imamura, Japanese voice actor
    - Roddy Piper, Canadian wrestler (d. 2015)
- April 22 – Jōji Nakata, Japanese voice actor
- April 23 – Michael Moore, American filmmaker/political activist
- April 27 – Herman Edwards, American football head coach
- April 28 – Michael Daugherty, American composer
- April 29
    - Jake Burton Carpenter, American founder of Burton Snowboards
    - Kazuko Kurosawa, Japanese costume designer
    - Jerry Seinfeld, American actor, comedian and producer

May

Johnny Logan

David Paterson

- May 1
    - Archie Norman, British politician and businessman
    - Ray Parker, Jr., American musician and composer (*Raydio*)
- May 2 – Elliot Goldenthal, American composer
- May 6 – Angela Hernández Nuñez, Dominican writer
- May 7
    - Philippe Geluck, Belgian cartoonist
    - Amy Heckerling, American film director
- May 8
    - Pam Arciero, *Sesame Street* puppeteer
    - John Michael Talbot, American Christian musician
    - Gary Wilmot, British entertainer
- May 13 – Johnny Logan, Australian-born Irish singer and composer, Eurovision Song Contest 1980, 1987 winner dubbed as "Mister Eurovision"
- May 19
    - Hōchū Ōtsuka, Japanese voice actor
    - Phil Rudd, Australian rock drummer (*AC/DC*)
- May 20 – David Paterson, American politician, Governor of New York

- May 22 – Shuji Nakamura, Japanese electronics engineer
- May 26 – Danny Rolling, American murderer (d. 2006)
- May 27
  - Pauline Hanson, Australian politician
  - Lawrence M. Krauss, American theoretical physicist and science writer

June

Will Patton

Jim Belushi

Kathleen Turner

Serzh Sargsyan

- June 2 – Chiyoko Kawashima, Retired Japanese voice actress
- June 4 – Kazuhiro Yamaji, Japanese actor and voice actor
- June 5 – Nancy Stafford, American actress and Christian author
- June 9
  - John Hagelin, American physicist and U.S. Presidential candidate
  - Elizabeth May, leader of the Green Party of Canada
- June 14 – Will Patton, American actor
- June 15
  - Jim Belushi, American actor (*Saturday Night Live*)
  - Bob McDonnell, American politician

- June 16 – Sergey Kuryokhin, Russian pianist, composer, improvisor, performance artist and actor (d. 1996)
- June 19
  - Ted Coombs, American artist
  - Kathleen Turner, American actress
- June 20
  - Michael Anthony, American rock bassist (*Van Halen*)
  - Karlheinz Brandenburg, German electrical engineer and mathematician
  - Ilan Ramon, Israeli Air Force fighter pilot and Israel's first astronaut (d. 2003)
- June 21 – Anne Kirkbride, British Actress (Coronation Street) (d. 2015)
- June 22 – Freddie Prinze, American actor and comedian (d. 1977)
- June 25 – Sonia Sotomayor, American Associate Justice of the Supreme Court
- June 26 – Steve Barton, American actor (d. 2001)
- June 27 – Ron Kirk, Mayor of Dallas, Texas
- June 28 – Ava Barber, American country singer (*The Lawrence Welk Show*)
- June 29 – Rick Honeycutt, American baseball player and coach
- June 30 – Pierre Charles, Prime Minister of Dominica (d. 2004)

July

Angela Merkel

Hugo Chávez

- July 2 – Peter Randall-Page, British artist
- July 5 – John Wright, New Zealand cricket captain
- July 6 – Willie Randolph, American baseball player, coach, manager
- July 10
    - Neil Tennant, British musician
    - Yō Yoshimura, Japanese voice actor (d. 1991)
- July 13 – Sezen Aksu, Turkish singer
- July 15
    - Tarak Dhiab, Tunisian footballer
    - Mario Kempes, Argentine footballer
- July 16 – Jeanette Mott Oxford, American politician

- July 17
  - Angela Merkel, current Chancellor of Germany
  - Eduardo Romero, Argentine golfer
  - J. Michael Straczynski, American author
- July 20 – Wilson Casey, American syndicated columnist and entertainer
- July 22 – Pierre Lebeau, Canadian actor
- July 24 – Jorge Jesus, Portuguese football player and coach
- July 25 – Walter Payton, African-American football player (d. 1999)
- July 26
  - Vitas Gerulaitis, American tennis player (d. 1994)
  - Leonardo Daniel, Mexican actor and director
- July 27
  - Philippe Alliot, French race car driver
  - Lynne Frederick, British actress (d. 1994)
- July 28 – Hugo Chávez, President of Venezuela (d. 2013)
- July 29 – Mark Gersmehl, American Christian musician

August

August 1

- Michael Badnarik, American software engineer and presidential candidate
- James Gleick, an American nonfiction author of several award-winning books.
- Junpei Morita, Japanese actor and voice actor
- August 4

- ○ François Valéry, French singer-songwriter and composer
  - ○ Dorottya Udvaros, Hungarian actress
  - ○ Uwe Wittwer, Swiss artist
- August 9 – Pete Thomas, American longtime drummer for the Elvis Costello band
- August 11 – Joe Jackson, British rock 'n' roll singer (*Steppin' Out*)
- August 12
  - ○ François Hollande, current President of France
  - ○ Sam J. Jones, American actor
  - ○ Pat Metheny, American jazz guitarist
- August 13 – Nico Assumpção, Brazilian bass fiddle player
- August 14
  - ○ Mark Fidrych, American baseball player (d. 2009)
  - ○ Stanley A. McChrystal, major U.S. Army general
- August 16 – James Cameron, Canadian-born film director
- August 17 – Anatoly Kudryavitsky, Russian-Irish writer
- August 20
  - ○ Tawn Mastrey, American disc jockey, music video producer (d. 2007)
  - ○ Al Roker, television personality, host
  - ○ Don Stark, American actor
- August 21
  - ○ Steve Smith, American drummer
  - ○ Ivan Stang, American author and publisher
- August 23 – Charles Busch, American director, writer, and actor
- August 24 – Philippe Cataldo, French singer
- August 25 – Elvis Costello, English singer-songwriter

- August 29 – István Cserháti, Hungarian keyboardist (d. 2005)
- August 30 – Alexander Lukashenko, the President of Belarus
- August 31 – Caroline Cossey, British model

September

Shinzō Abe

- September 1 – Dave Lumley, Canadian ice hockey player
- September 7 – Michael Emerson, American actor
- September 10 – Mark W. Everson, American businessman; 46th Commissioner of the Internal Revenue Service (2003–07)
- September 13 – Steve Kilbey, Australian musician
- September 17 – Joël-François Durand, French composer
- September 18 – Dennis Johnson, American basketball player (d. 2007)
- September 21
  - Shinzō Abe, current Prime Minister of Japan
  - Thomas S. Ray, American ecologist
  - Phil "Philthy Animal" Taylor, English drummer (Motörhead and Waysted)

- September 24 – Lilian Mercedes Letona, Salvadoran guerrilla (d. 1983)
- September 26 – Kevin Kennedy, American baseball manager and television host
- September 28 – Steve Largent, American football player and congressman
- September 30 – Barry Williams, American actor

October

Ang Lee

Scott Bakula

- October 1 – Martin Strel, Slovenian swimmer
- October 3
    - Eddie DeGarmo, American Christian keyboardist and producer

- Dennis Eckersley, American baseball player
- Al Sharpton, African-American political activist
- Stevie Ray Vaughan, American musician (d. 1990)
- October 5 – Wayne Watson, American Christian musician
- October 6 – Howard Hoffman, American voice actor
- October 7 – Robert A. Schuller, American televangelist and the son of Robert H. Schuller
- October 9
  - Scott Bakula, American actor (*Quantum Leap*, *Star Trek: Enterprise*)
  - John O'Hurley, American actor and game show host
- October 10
  - Mohamed Mounir, Egyptian singer and actor
  - David Lee Roth, American rock singer
- October 12 – Linval Thompson, Jamaican singer and producer
- October 13 – Mordechai Vanunu, a former Israeli nuclear technician who revealed secrets of its nuclear weapons program
- October 15
  - Peter Bakowski, Australian poet
  - Michael Garner, English actor
- October 18 – Yūji Mitsuya, Japanese voice actor
- October 23 – Ang Lee, Taiwanese film director
- October 24
  - Doug Davidson, American actor
  - Mike Rounds, South Dakota politician
- October 30
  - Kathleen Cody, American actress
  - Mario Testino, Peruvian photographer

November

Condoleezza Rice

Aleksander Kwaśniewski

- November 2 – Angela Webber, Australian author, television writer, producer and comedian (d. 2007)
- November 3
  - Adam Ant, English singer
  - Kathy Kinney, American actress and comedian
  - Brigitte Lin, Taiwanese actress
- November 7
  - Robin Beck, American singer
  - Kamal Haasan, Indian actor
- November 8
  - Michael D. Brown, first Undersecretary of Emergency Preparedness and Response, a division of the United States' Department of Homeland Security

- Kazuo Ishiguro, Japanese-born British author
- November 12 – Rhonda Shear, American TV hostess, actress, and comedian
- November 13 – Chris Noth, American actor
- November 14
  - Willie Hernández, Puerto Rican Major League Baseball player
  - Bernard Hinault, French road bicycle racer
  - Condoleezza Rice, former U.S. Secretary of State
  - Yanni, Greek musician
- November 15 – Aleksander Kwaśniewski, President of Poland
- November 16 – Bruce Edwards, American golf caddy (d. 2004)
- November 18 – John Parr, English singer and musician
- November 19 – Abdel Fattah el-Sisi, President of Egypt
- November 23 – Bruce Hornsby, American rock singer
- November 26
  - Roz Chast, American cartoonist
  - Dan Kwong, American performance artist, playwright
- November 27
  - Patricia McPherson, American actress
  - Kimmy Robertson, American actress
- November 29 – Joel Coen, American film director, producer, screenwriter, and editor

December

Ray Liotta

Annie Lennox

Denzel Washington

- December 1 – Bob Goen, American television personality and game show host
- December 2 – Stone Phillips, American television journalist

- December 3 – Grace Andreacchi, American author
- December 4 – Tony Todd, American actor and producer
- December 6 – Beat Furrer, Swiss-born Austrian composer and conductor
- December 7 – Mark Hofmann, American forger and murderer
- December 10 – Jack Hues, English singer and musician (Wang Chung)
- December 11
    - Sylvester Clarke, West Indian cricketer (d. 1999)
    - Jermaine Jackson, African-American singer
    - Prachanda, Nepalese Communist leader
- December 13 – John Anderson, American country music singer-songwriter
- December 14
    - Ib Andersen, Danish dancer
    - Alan Kulwicki, American race car driver (d. 1993)
- December 15 – Mark Warner, American politician
- December 18
    - Ray Liotta, American actor
    - Uli Jon Roth, German rock guitarist (*Scorpions*)
- December 20 – Sandra Cisneros, American writer
- December 21 – Chris Evert, American tennis player
- December 24 – José María Figueres, Costa Rican politician, President 1994–1998
- December 25 – Annie Lennox, British rock singer (*Eurythmics*)
- December 26
    - Susan Butcher, American dog-sled racer (d. 2006)
    - Ozzie Smith, HOF baseball shortstop

- December 28
  - Lanny Poffo, American professional wrestler
  - Denzel Washington, African-American actor
- December 29 – Albrecht Böttcher, German mathematician
- December 31 – Alex Salmond, Scottish politician

Deaths

January

- January 5
  - Rabbit Maranville, American baseball player (Boston Braves) and a member of the MLB Hall of Fame (b. 1891)
  - Lillian Rich, English actress (b. 1900)
- January 8 – Eduard Wiiralt, Estonian artist (b. 1898)
- January 11 – Oscar Straus, Austrian composer (b. 1870)
- January 12 – William H. P. Blandy, American admiral (b. 1890)
- January 18 – Sydney Greenstreet, English actor (b. 1879)
- January 20 – Fred Root, English cricketer (b. 1890)
- January 30
  - John Murray Anderson, Canadian theater director and producer (b. 1886)
  - Dorothy Price, Irish physician (b. 1890)
- January 31
  - Edwin Armstrong, American electrical engineer (b. 1890)
  - Florence Bates, American actress (b. 1888)

February

- February 6 – Maxwell Bodenheim, American poet and novelist (murdered) (b. 1892)
- February 8 – Laurence Trimble, American actor (b. 1885)

- February 9 – Mabel Paige, American actress (b. 1880)
- February 11 – Thomas Pierrepoint, British executioner (b. 1870)
- February 12 – Dziga Vertov, Russian filmmaker (b. 1896)
- February 21 – William K. Howard, American film director (b. 1899)

March

Otto Diels

- March 7
  - Otto Diels, German chemist, Nobel Prize laureate (b. 1876)
  - Will H. Hays, Namesake for the Hays Code (b. 1879)
- March 9 – Vagn Walfrid Ekman, Swedish oceanographer (b. 1874)
- March 26 – Louis Silvers, American film composer (b. 1889)
- March 30 – Horatio Dresser, American writer (b. 1866)

April

- April 8 – Fritzi Scheff, actress & singer (b. 1879)
- April 10 – Auguste Lumière, French film pioneer (b. 1862)

- April 12 – Luis Cabrera Lobato, Mexican lawyer, politician and writer (b. 1876)
- April 13 – Angus L. Macdonald, Nova Scotia Premier (b. 1890)
- April 15 – Ülo Altermann, Estonian soldier and forest brother (b. 1923)
- April 17 – Lucrețiu Pătrășcanu, Romanian communist activist and sociologist (b. 1900)
- April 28 – Léon Jouhaux, French labor leader, recipient of the Nobel Peace Prize (b. 1879)
- April 29
  - Kathleen Clarice Groom, British writer (b. 1872)
  - Joe May, Austrian-born director (b. 1880)

May

- May 1 – Tom Tyler, American actor (b. 1903)
- May 3 – Józef Garbień, Polish footballer and physician (b. 1896)
- May 6 – B. C. Forbes, Scottish-born publisher (b. 1880)
- May 14 – Heinz Guderian, German World War II general (b. 1888)
- May 15 – William March, American writer and soldier (b. 1893)
- May 19 – Charles Ives, American composer (b. 1874)
- May 22 – Chief Bender, Native-American baseball player (Philadelphia Athletics) and a member of the MLB Hall of Fame (b. 1884)
- May 25 – Robert Capa, Hungarian-born photojournalist (b. 1913)

June

Alan Turing

- June 7 – Alan Turing, British mathematician, cryptanalyst, and pioneer computer scientist (b. 1912)
- June 22 – Don Hollenbeck, American newscaster (b. 1905)

July

Frida Kahlo

- July 1 – Thea von Harbou, German actress (b. 1888)
- July 3 – Reginald Marsh, American artist (b. 1898)
- July 6 – Gabriel Pascal, Hungarian producer and director (b. 1894)
- July 11 – Henry Valentine Knaggs, English physician and author (b. 1859)
- July 13

- Frida Kahlo, Mexican painter (b. 1907)
- Irving Pichel, American actor and director (b. 1891)
- Grantland Rice, American sportswriter (b. 1880)
- July 14
  - Jacinto Benavente, Spanish writer, Nobel Prize laureate (b. 1866)
  - Jackie Saunders, American silent screen actress (b. 1892)
- July 16 – Herms Niel, German composer (b. 1888)
- July 17 – Machine Gun Kelly, American gangster (b. 1895)
- July 28 – Sōjin Kamiyama or "Sojin", Japanese film star during the American silent film era, (b. 1884)
- July 29 – Coen de Koning, Dutch speed skater (b. 1879)

August

- August 3
  - Bess Streeter Aldrich, American writer (b. 1881)
  - Colette, French novelist (b. 1873)
- August 14 – Hugo Eckener, President of the Zeppelin Dirigible Company (b. 1868)
- August 19 – Alcide De Gasperi, Italian statesman and politician (b. 1881)
- August 24 – Getúlio Vargas, President of Brazil (b. 1882)
- August 31 – Elsa Barker, American writer (b. 1869)

September

- September 1 – Bert Acosta, American aviator (b. 1895)
- September 3 – Eugene Pallette, American actor (b. 1889)
- September 5 – Eugen Schiffer, German politician (b. 1860)

- September 6 – Edward C. Kalbfus, American admiral (b. 1877)
- September 7
  - Bud Fisher, American cartoonist (b. 1885)
  - Glenn Scobey Warner, American college football coach (b. 1871)
- September 21 – Mikimoto Kōkichi, Japanese pearl farm pioneer (b. 1858)
- September 24 – Edward Pilgrim, British homeowner (suicide) (b. 1904)
- September 27 – Maximilian von Weichs, German field marshal (b. 1881)
- September 28 – Bert Lytell, American actor (b. 1885)

October

Enrico Fermi

- October 9 – Robert H. Jackson, United States Supreme Court associate justice and chief prosecutor at the Nuremberg Trials (b. 1892)
- October 12 – George Welch, American aviator (b. 1918)
- October 19 – Hugh Duffy, American baseball player (Boston Braves) and a member of the MLB Hall of Fame (b. 1866)

- October 22 – Jibanananda Das, Indian poet, writer, novelist and essayist in Bengali (b. 1899)
- October 30 – Wilbur Shaw, American racing driver (b. 1902)

November

Henri Matisse

Wilhelm Furtwängler

- November 3 – Henri Matisse, French painter (b. 1869)
- November 13 – Paul Ludwig Ewald von Kleist, German field marshal (b. 1881)
- November 15 – Lionel Barrymore, American actor (b. 1878)
- November 16 – Albert Francis Blakeslee, American botanist (b. 1874)
- November 17 – Yitzhak Lamdan, Russian-born Israeli poet and columnist (b. 1899)

- November 20 – Clyde Vernon Cessna, American pilot and aircraft designer, founded the Cessna Aircraft Corporation (b. 1879)
- November 22
    - Roderick McMahon, American professional boxing and wrestling promoter; founder of Capitol Wrestling Corporation (b.1882)
    - Moroni Olsen, American actor (b. 1889)
    - Andrey Vyshinsky, Russian jurist and diplomat (b. 1883)
- November 28 – Enrico Fermi, Italian physicist, Nobel Prize laureate (b. 1901)
- November 29 – Dink Johnson, American musician (b. 1892)
- November 30 – Wilhelm Furtwängler, German conductor (b. 1886)

December

- December 1 – Fred Rose, American songwriter (b. 1898)
- December 8
    - Claude Cahun, French photographer and writer (b. 1894
    - Gladys George, American actress (b. 1904)
- December 20 – James Hilton, English novelist (b. 1900)
- December 23 – René Iché, French sculptor (b. 1897)
- December 27 – Adolph Otto Niedner, American cartridge designer (b. 1863)
- December 30 –
    - Archduke Eugen of Austria, Austrian field marshal (b. 1863)

- Günther Quandt, German industrialist who founded an industrial empire that today includes BMW and Altana (b. 1881)

Nobel Prizes

- Physics – Max Born, Walther Bothe
- Chemistry – Linus Pauling
- Medicine – John Franklin Enders, Thomas Huckle Weller, Frederick Chapman Robbins
- Literature – Ernest Hemingway
- Peace – The Office of the United Nations High Commissioner for Refugees.

In the News.

Jan 10th A Comet jet airliner crashes in the Mediterranea; 35 people are missing.

Jan 22nd 11th Golden Globes: The Robe, Spencer Tracy, & Audrey Hepburn win.

Mar 1st US explodes Castle Bravo, 15 megaton hydrogen bomb at Bikini Atoll - most powerful nuclear device ever detonated by the US.

Mar 19th 1st color telecast of a prize fight, Giardello vs Troy in Madison Square Garden, NYC.

Apr 2nd Plans to build Disneyland 1st announced.

Apr 5th Elvis Presley records his debut single "That's All Right"

Apr 12th Bill Haley & Comets records "Rock Around Clock"

May 6th Roger Bannister of Britain breaks 4 minute mile (3:59:4)

Jun 17th Rocky Marciano beats Ezzard Charles in 15 for heavyweight boxing title.

Jul 3rd Food rationing ends in Britain.

Jul 5th The BBC broadcasts its first television news bulletin.

Sep 29th "Star is Born" starring Judy Garland & James Mason premieres.

Nov 24th Air Force One, 1st US Presidential airplane, christened.

Dec 4th The first Burger King is opened in Miami, Florida, USA.

Inventions - Oral contraceptives the pill - The first nonstick teflon pan produced. - The solar cell invented by Chaplin, Fuller and Pearson. And Ray Kroc started McDonalds.